A SIMPLE OUTLINE OF GOD'S WAY OF SALVATION

DO I NEED TO BE SAVED?

God is holy. No sin will ever enter his presence, for "righteousness and justice are the foundation of his throne" (Psalm 97:2).

Humanity is sinful. "For all have sinned and fall short of the glory of God" (Romans 3:23).

Sin separates all people from God. "Your iniquities have made a separation between you and your God, and your sins have hidden his face from you" (Isaiah 59:2).

It is impossible for humans to save themselves. "By works of the law no human being will be justified in his sight" (Romans 3:20).

CAN I BE SAVED?

God sent his Son to be your Savior. "In this is love, not that we have loved God but that he loved us and sent his Son to be the propitiation for our sins" (1 John 4:10).

The living Savior invites sinners to receive him. "Come to me, all who labor and are heavy laden, and I will give you rest" (Matthew 11:28).

Forgiveness of sins and salvation can be yours today. "For Christ also suffered once for sins, the righteous for the unrighteous, that he might bring us to God" (1 Peter 3:18).

HOW CAN I BE SAVED?

Agree with God that you are a lost sinner unable to save yourself. "God shows his love for us in that while we were still sinners, Christ died for us" (Romans 5:8).

Believe that Jesus Christ died for your sins and ask him to be your Savior. "To all who did receive him, who believed in his name, he gave the right to become children of God" (John 1:12).

Confess the Lord Jesus Christ. "If you confess with your mouth that Jesus is Lord and believe in your heart that God raised him from the dead, you will be saved" (Romans 10:9).

"Truly, truly, I say to you, whoever hears my word and believes him who sent me has eternal life. He does not come into judgment, but has passed from death to life" (John 5:24).

CROSSWAY | **GOOD NEWS** *Tracts*

goodnewstracts.org

ISBN 978-1-68216-311-5